THE ARMORY

TEENS

THE ARMORY
TEENS

Printed by IngramSpark

ISBN-13: 979-8-218-47529-1

ACKNOWLEDGEMENTS

The Valor™ series, including its booklets and workbooks, has been the product of ongoing clinical and coaching work with teens and college-aged young men since 2007. I am grateful for the courage of these young men as they worked through personal challenges. They've provided immense insight into various clinical issues. I also cannot ignore the insights of adults in our SA program who suggested the Valor group – wishing they'd had something similar when they were younger.

THE ARMORY

TEENS

Contents

THE ARMORY

Whether in an ancient castle or a modern military base, an Armory is a special place set aside to safely store weapons and tools for battle. These weapons and tools are used to protect and defend from an enemy attack. This booklet represents your personal "Armory" in your battle against pornography or sexual problems. It teaches basic tools and weapons you can utilize when you need to fight. None of the weapons or tools are magical… so you'll have to push yourself and work hard. They are only as effective as your effort. You can do this!

WELCOME

Congrats on joining a Valor™ group! It takes courage to admit that you need help, and it shows commitment as you jump into a group. The objective of your Valor group is to work together, to share and support one another, so that everyone succeeds. Overcoming problems with pornography or sexual issues requires support. No one succeeds in isolation!

You'll receive workbooks throughout the program and will be doing group activities to help you learn. It might feel weird at first to talk about embarrassing topics, but it's worth it. Don't let fear hold you back. Lean in and trust the guys in your group. This is a team effort!

This Armory booklet contains tools and weapons to keep you on track. While there's no magic fix, these tools have helped many young men. Put them to use and decide what works best for you. As part of the Valor group, we also look out for each other. Sometimes you'll be the one teaching new guys how to use these tools, and other times, you'll be sharing what's worked best for you. It's all about supporting each other.

If you want success… make sure you focus on the small wins every day! If you stop trying whenever you get discouraged, you're not going to win. Learn to get back up and shake it off. Once you start winning more than you lose, you're on the path to victory. At first it might feel impossible to be self-disciplined and manage the feelings and urges. It's not impossible… but takes practice. You'll get stronger over time if you don't give up. Don't get discouraged. Just keep getting back up every time. Whenever you're feeling low, it's super important to reach out to someone for a pep talk and encouragement.

True change comes from inside you. It's more than just avoiding slips. You'll be moving up through different ranks in this program, and each rank is built around key areas you've got to work through. If you're aiming for lasting success, you need to improve yourself in each area.

Key Topics

Everything you learn in Valor™ will revolve around eight basic topics. These are topics that most counselors and coaches will refer to when creating an intervention to help you. These key topics are essential to make sure you approach the problem from every angle. We'll talk more about these with you and your parents and as you read and complete the workbooks.

1. Support Network Development

2. Toxic-Shame Reduction

3. Recovery Education

4. Social Skill Development

5. Sobriety Skill Improvement

6. Self-Esteem Development

7. Family System Enhancement

8. Emotional Awareness

We don't need to talk about these items right now, but wanted to list them so you know what they are. If you have questions, talk to your counselor or coach. Each of these key areas will be addressed throughout your time in Valor.

Habit or Compulsion or Addiction?

The first order of business is to decide whether your issue with porn has become a habit… or has escalated into a compulsion or addiction. You've probably noticed how easy it is to start watching porn. Sometimes it begins as curiosity and then gets out of control. What starts as a few minutes quickly turns into hours. But how do you tell if this is just a bad habit or if it's starting to mess with your life? Let's break it down.

A **habit** is something you do often, almost without thinking about it. A **compulsion** is when you can't stop yourself and feel out of control with the porn. An **addiction** is when you can't function without using it; you feel like you need it to feel okay or normal. Talk to your counselor or coach about your own situation. Many teens are struggling with porn because its a habit or a compulsion, not necessarily because they are addicted. However, to keep things in the program simple we are going to use the word addiction to describe the problem when its out of control. But remember, this doesn't necessarily mean you are addicted.

The following list contains common questions to ask yourself about whether you might be addicted. Check it out and discuss these with your counselor or coach:

1. Need for More:

Ever noticed needing more screen time to get the same 'high'? That's your brain asking for a higher dose. Are you slowly, over time, using it more often for longer periods of time? If you can't put it down and you think you're losing self-control, you might be developing an addiction.

2. Life Takes a Hit:

Are your grades, job, relationships, sports activities, or friend groups sliding because you're too caught up watching porn? In other words, are you spending time using porn when you should be doing other important things? If so, you could be addicted.

3. Negative Vibes:

Has watching porn got you feeling bad about yourself? Has it started to erode your confidence and self-esteem? Do you ever hate yourself afterwards?

4. Can't Quit:

Tried to cut down or stop but couldn't? That's an addiction knocking on your door. Do you feel like you "need" it?

5. Mood Swings:

Using porn to chill from stress or getting cranky when you can't watch it? Do you turn to porn when you are depressed, anxious, bored, lonely, stressed or generally feeling bad? Do you feel like you need it to cope with emotions?

6. **Values or Morals:**
   Have you found that watching porn and the things you are viewing conflicts with personal values or morals? Do you promise others or God that you'll stop, but then you keep going back to it?

7. **Withdrawal:**
   Do you try to stop using porn but find that you have withdrawal symptoms? For example: you can't sleep, feel restless, get irritable, have body aches or headaches, feel moody, get depressed or your testicles hurt?

If any of the above applies to you, you might be addicted. Be honest with yourself. When habits become an addiction, it slowly destroys your life. The danger with addiction is that it usually escalates and gets worse over time.

Whether it's just a bad habit or has become an addiction, don't be embarrassed! Either way, there's always hope. The key is a decision to make a change. The concepts in the Valor series will teach you what you need to know.

Bottom Lines

As you start using the Armory, you've got to establish "bottom lines." These are your "no-go zones." These bottom lines are behaviors you're trying to stop. Take Kyle for instance who created the following bottom lines:

> 1. I will not masturbate.
> 2. I will not look at pornography.
> 3. I will not have sex with my girlfriend.

Once you've established "bottom lines," find someone you can share them with. Let this person know these are the behaviors you're trying to stop. Remember this is what you're striving for.

Personal Rules

After your bottom lines are in place, your next step will be to generate personal rules. These rules help to maintain your bottom lines. Personal rules aren't about cutting off temptation - they're about keeping you further away from it. Personal rules help to keep you away from risky situations.

Here's Matthew's Personal Rules:

1. Take short five-minute showers.
2. Only use my laptop when someone else is around.
3. Ask my dad to check my phone history every night.
4. Keep my phone out of my room at bedtime.
5. Never take my girlfriend into my bedroom.

Recovery vs Sobriety

If you've become addicted, we'll often talk about recovery and sobriety. Sobriety means you're not acting out sexually. When someone asks if you're sober, they're asking if you've crossed any bottom lines. You're NOT "sober" if you've slipped into a sexual behavior you're trying to stop.

Keep in mind, staying sober is not the same as recovery. You could stop all sexual activity and still not be in recovery. Staying sober is about managing your body's impulses to stop acting out. Recovery is about changing what's inside you so that sobriety happens naturally. When you handle your needs in a healthy way, the bad habits naturally fade away. Recovery is about reshaping your life from the inside, doing things that might not feel easy at first. If you're working with a counselor or coach, they will guide you. Just remember, there's a big difference between staying sober and living recovery.

Triggers

Whether it's a bad habit or you're addicted, your first objective is to get sober. How do you do this? You've got to learn about your triggers. A trigger is anything that sets into motion your sexual thoughts and behavior. It gets you moving closer to your bottom lines. Recognizing triggers can empower you! When you see them coming, you can prepare tools to escape the situation.

Understanding your triggers will help you regain control. It's about preparing yourself ahead of time. There are mainly three types of triggers. Discuss these with your counselor or coach so you can be clear about how it applies to you. Remember triggers aren't bad, they simply cause your brain to start moving toward sexual thoughts, feelings, and behavior. The following are a list of the three categories of triggers:

1. Sensory

2. Emotional

3. Situational

Sensory

These triggers are things you see, hear, taste, touch, or smell.

Check out some examples:

- *The smell of perfume in math class triggers Keyton.*

- *Trevor gets triggered walking down the hallway when girls accidentally brush his arm.*

- *When he goes to the beach, William gets triggered seeing the girls in bikinis.*

Emotional

These are feelings like sadness, anger, fear, happiness, or embarrassment. This includes feeling depressed, frustrated, rejected, alone, stressed, overwhelmed, or just plain bored.

For instance:

- *Zach gets angry when he argues with his mom and just stews in his room.*

- *Rejection by kids at school upsets Tyler.*

- *Kyle gets antsy when he's bored doing homework.*

Situational

These are specific places, times, or scenarios.

For example:

- *Brandon gets triggered during Christmas break when there's no schedule.*

- *Brock's friend's house where he first saw porn now triggers him.*

- *Zane finds it tough when he's home alone, by himself.*

Don't be afraid of having triggers. It's about responding strategically. You'll be empowered when you understand your own triggers. They aren't bad, but often lead toward sexual temptation that will cross your bottom lines.

Tools & Weapons

Once you establish bottom lines, create some personal rules, and understand triggers, it's time to start using tools and weapons in your battle against temptation.

As you learn learn and practice various tools and weapons to stay sober, we encourage you to make time with a mental health counselor or coach. They can help you deal with personal issues as needed. Make sure you talk with them about your strategies to stay sober. It's key to figure out which tools work for you and when to use them. Since everyone is different, a strategy that's a game-changer for you might not do much for someone else.

If you want to be successful, implement strategies *every single day.* Even on days when you're not struggling… keep practicing. Just because you're not feeling the urge, doesn't mean you should stop practicing your tools. For example, if you're learning to reach out for support, call someone daily regardless of whether you're struggling or not. You need to practice reaching out every day.

Chat with your counselor or coach about the key topics of the Valor series. Keep your parents or a mentor involved. Effective recovery for dealing with compulsive sexual behavior is typically centered around eight core principles. Tackle each area with your counselor or coach during your private sessions.

What's your starting point? Get sober! Learn to stop acting out. It's tough in the beginning, but we're confident these concepts will help.

Strengthening your sobriety also implies you are creating a support team. Ideally, this would include your parents, trusted adults, or friends who are mature. We'll talk more about a support team later.

As you make progress, you'll become more in tune with your emotions by taking part in Valor group activities and working through individual struggles with your counselor or coach. Whenever you need a boost, come back and read through this Armory. Have courage and keep moving forward!

NOTES

TOOLS & WEAPONS

Using the Tools

The tools and weapons within this next section will give you traction to win the battles you've been fighting. Practice them daily and share them with your parents, mentor, counselor, or coach. Remember, these tools and weapons are not magical! They require effort. You'll have to push yourself when uncomfortable, to use various tools or weapons at difficult times. The harder you push, the better the tools and weapons will work. You've got this!

Personal Rules

Personal rules are simple. Create some basic guidelines or "rules" about things to do which keep you further away from triggers and temptations. You'll want to make these personal rules a habit. These would be things you do every day without fail. They're not going to wipe out difficulty, but it helps to reduce the pressure.

For instance, Liam decided his personal rules would include the following:

- Keep showers under 7 minutes.
- Never bring laptop into my room.
- Hang out in groups, no solo dates.
- Charge my phone in the kitchen at bedtime.
- Phone is not allowed in the bathroom.

In these examples, Liam's rules steer him further away from temptation. Now, it's your turn. What rules would be helpful to you? You might want to run ideas by your mentor, parents, counselor, or coach. They might also have suggestions that could help.

1. _______________________

2. _______________________

3. _______________________

4. _______________________

5. _______________________

6. _______________________

Reach Out

This tool might seem super basic, but is one of the most help-ful things you can do! It's the absolute best way to help yourself when things get tough. A lot of teens find it hard to openly talk about personal issues. Feeling embarrassed or ashamed makes it awkward to tell someone you're struggling. However, to be real with someone about what you're going through is healing. The guys who do the best are the ones who don't hesitate to reach out, even when everything seems fine. Try to make this a daily habit to keep yourself on track. This is about transparency.

Reaching out means calling or texting someone - any way you can communicate. Remember, the gold standard is ALWAYS going to be talking face-to-face. Hanging out and having a real talk is the best. If you can't physically go over to someone's house, the next best thing is to talk on the phone. Other ways to connect, like texting or social media are still good, but not the best.

Call the guys from your Valor group. Lean on friends who aren't judgmental or a mentor who can support you. Be cautious with friends who aren't mature - especially the ones who can't keep information private or who stir up gossip and drama. If you're not sure who might be safe, talk it over with your counselor or coach for better insight.

Write down three names of people you can reach out to.

Accountability Partner

This tool is like checking in, but more planned out. Basically, you set up a regular meetup with someone to chat about how you're doing. This could be a mentor, trusted adult, someone from the Valor group, or a parent. We would suggest you talk about these items:

- *How have you been feeling **physically?** (e.g., sick, tired, energetic)*

- *How have you been feeling **emotionally?** (e.g., anxious, stressed, angry)*

- *How are you doing **spiritually** in your connection to God?*

- *Any difficult **triggers** that have occurred.*

- *Did you cross any **bottom lines?***

- *Explain the **tools or weapons** you've been using.*

Just grab someone and ask if they'd be available to meet up for some accountability. Try to do this at least once a week.

3-Second Stop

This tool is about stopping sexual thoughts within three seconds. The longer you dwell on these thoughts, the tougher it is to move away from them. Within a few seconds, your brain starts pumping out chemicals that work against you, pushing you closer to acting on those thoughts. The more you dwell on them, the more your body leans into the urges, and the harder it is to pull away.

Since your sexual thoughts seemed out of control in the past, catching and quickly dropping those thoughts is key. It's totally normal to have sexual urges, but learn to manage them quickly to maintain control. Young men in high school and college have growing sexual urges that are natural and normal. Don't shame yourself about sexual curiosity, but learn to manage it.

Fast Forward

Have you ever been caught up with porn or sex and felt hypnotized? Like, as if your brain's just stuck there, and shaking it off feels impossible? When that happens, your daydreams might get vivid. The Fast Forward tool can help. Instead of dwelling on the fantasy, pause and play your thoughts into the future. Think about the aftermath of slipping. Ask yourself a few questions:

- *Right after I give in, how's that going to make me feel?*

- *Will I have any regrets later?*

- *Have I promised anyone I'd report to them when I slip?*

- *How's it going to feel when I report to them?*

- *When I've slipped in the past how does it make me feel?*

- *Will slipping postpone any of the goals I've set for myself?*

You can even take it to the next level and imagine the worst-case ending. For example:

- *Could things get worse from here? Could the problem be escalating?*

- *Is it possible I might slip and get caught? What would the person who catches me think?*

- *If things get worse, who else gets dragged down with me?*

- *Could this ruin my future plans or dreams?*

- *Could this next slip create problems in dating or social relationships?*

- *Is there anyone who might be disappointed?*

- *Could this lead me to giving up? Could this draw me into depression, anxiety or shame?*

Thinking ahead about real consequences and what could happen, can actually help dial down that temptation. Simply fast-forward to after the slip.

Ammo Box

When soldiers move into battle they bring an ammo box. This is filled with supplies to reload their weapons. Without this container, they'd run out of ammunition and be stranded on the battlefield without protection.

Think of your struggle against sexual problems like an epic battle. There will be times you're running low on ammunition and need a way to "reload." This tool creates an ammo box filled with items to help you reload when you're tired and running low.

Get a shoe box or container and fill it with items that boost your mood and bring to mind good things about yourself. These items will remind you about why you are fighting this battle. They could be music, photos, letters, awards, certificates, scripture verses, or anything that holds special value for you. Use items that lift your spirit and give you confidence.

Chat with your parents, counselor, or coach to figure out what to place inside your box to make it encouraging and helpful. When difficult times arise or you're feeling down, pull out your ammo box and look through each item to reload your enthusiasm.

For example, Ezra put the following items in his Ammo Box:

- Picture of my Uncle Robert, he's rooting for me.
- Certificate I've earned from Track.
- Letter grandpa gave me before he died.
- Picture of me and Uncle Robert.
- Picture of me and my best friend.
- Note my buddy gave me.
- Paper with our Valor group names and cell numbers.
- Autographed baseball from Pete Rose.

Shake It Off

Slipping back into habits and crossing bottom lines is discouraging with all the guilt that piles up. It can send you back into toxic shame. However, beating yourself up with shame doesn't help. It's like adding weight to a backpack while running a marathon. You have to shake off the shame and bounce back. Try this tool to shake off the shame messages in your head. Simply answer the four questions. You can do this on a sheet of paper whenever you need it.

Here's an example of how Andrew used this tool to "shake it off":

It's true that…	I just looked at porn again.
But that doesn't mean…	that I'm a bad person, or I have to be embarrassed.
What's true is that…	a lot of guys my age are struggling with porn. It's difficult.
I like myself because…	I'm trying really hard, just like when I'm on the swim team. I push myself hard. I'm strong, not weak.

It's true that…	
But that doesn't mean…	
What's true is that…	
I like myself because…	

Move the Phone

Do most of your slips happen with your phone? This weapon is simple: put your phone somewhere else when you're not using it. You might feel like you've got to have your phone 24/7, but honestly there are moments during the day when you really don't need it. This is especially true at bedtime. Research shows that cutting out screen time 30 minutes before bed leads to better sleep - whether it's your phone, tablet, or TV. Trust me, you'll notice the difference.

Plan to move your phone at bedtime. Maybe check it in with your parents or find a specific spot somewhere else in the house. It will help you to dodge late-night struggles. If you're worried about an alarm clock, simply go buy one at the store. They're cheap and will wake you up without any additional notifications. The main point here is to move your phone so you don't have such quick and easy access to it.

Secure the Computer

It's pretty crucial to have blocks and filters on the devices you're using, especially your computer. There are a couple of ways to make that happen. First, you could set up a filter for your entire network. This means changing the settings on the household router. You can use free services like OpenDNS to block unwanted stuff for anyone who's connected to your Wi-Fi. Or you might consider getting a router that's already set up to filter content - like Clean Router or Barracuda. This would require that you talk to your parents or a trusted adult to make it happen.

Another option is putting a filter directly on your own laptop or the family computer. There are a bunch of options out there. Again, teaming up with someone who knows their way around technology can make this a lot easier. A lot of guys will use something like Covenant Eyes.

Remember with any block or filter, nothing is foolproof. They only give you a barrier which makes it easier to stay sober.

Secure the Phone

Having a phone filter is vital in this battle. Grab someone you trust—could be a mentor or parent —head into your phone settings and restrictions, then lock down any specific sites or content. Only the trusted person you've chosen should know the password. This is about keeping you focused, not locked out.

If your phone's got a web browser, turn it off. Instead, check out apps like Covenant Eyes that provide a safer way to browse online. It might require a small fee, but it's worth it. Recovery is about making smart moves to keep you on track.

If you've got some apps that create temptation, team up with someone to place a "restriction" on your phone to require "permission" to download or delete apps. This way, you can't download or eliminate apps without this other person knowing. It might feel annoying, but it's better than slipping across one of your bottom lines. You can still get the apps you want after your chosen person gives you the green light. This keeps you on track and makes sure you've got someone looking out for you.

Accountability Apps

As long as you're installing filters or blocks on your phone or computer, you should also consider installing an accountability app. This would be something like Covenant Eyes that will automatically send your accountability partners a notification when you're having trouble. It tracks your online behavior and sends notifications. Obviously, you'd need to choose some adults or friends that are willing to hold you accountable every time they receive a negative report. However, having an actual person check in with you about your search history is incredibly helpful.

Dumb Phone

Sometimes the phone is the biggest struggle. Even with filters and blockers, it might be overwhelming. If this is your situation, talk to your parents or someone you trust about trading in your phone for a period of time, to get a "dumb phone" or a flip phone. This could be for 30 days, 60 days, or 90 days. Choose the amount of time you need to get a handle on your phone use. These phones will have VERY limited or zero online access. In most cases they only allow texting, phone calls and basic needs.

Warrior Pose

Use this tool to change your mindset. Quickly straighten your posture and sit up straight. Pull your shoulders back or stand tall with your head up. Pose yourself as if you were a warrior or a soldier. Put on some good hype music that gets you feeling happy or pumped. Take a few minutes during the music to imagine yourself as tough; to see yourself as successful and strong! Envision yourself winning the battle against these problems and full of confidence!

Create a few positive phrases you can say when you take a warrior pose. For example, Karter created these phrases:

- *I am stronger than this temptation!*
- *I resist what my body wants.*
- *I push myself hard to achieve the goals I want!*
- *Pain is my friend.*

Now create some phrases that might work for you:

Messages

Are there positive or encouraging messages that are meaningful to you? Maybe your mentor or a teacher said something that made you feel good about yourself. Maybe there's a famous quote that's inspiring. Write these on post-it notes and place them around your room, in your car, around your house, in your locker at school, on your laptop, or in your backpack. Put them in places you will see them frequently.

Look at the example of messages that Hunter put in his room and his locker at school:

> - I don't have to be perfect to be good enough!
> - I have friends who love me just the way I am!
> - My brother knows about my stuff and still thinks I'm awesome!
> - Real men are the ones who never give up.

Vision Board

This tool requires a couple weeks to complete. Grab something sturdy like a small poster board, cardboard, or thick paper. It could be something used for science projects when you were a kid (but smaller). Sketch or glue pictures onto it that you've printed, to show all the awesome benefits about living recovery. You can also use words or short sentences. It's like creating a collage of the life you want. You've got to be able to imagine in your mind where you're headed and all the benefits that will follow. This tool helps you physically create the imagery that up until now has only been in your head.

As you consider various images or pictures for the board, review the following questions. Write your thoughts down before you dive into creating your vision board:

- *How's recovery going to change things at home?*

- *What will recovery do for your friendships, social life, or dating?*

- *How's it going to impact your family, or the future family you hope to create?*

- *Imagine the new activities you'll enjoy. What will change?*

- *Will anything change with your spiritual life?*

- *How will things be different with your parents, siblings or friends?*

- *How will sobriety boost your confidence or self-esteem?*

- *Will you become more outgoing, more adventurous, or more social?*

Keep these questions in mind as you build your Vision Board. This will be like your guide to visualizing a future that you're working to achieve.

Shadow Board

This is the opposite of the Vision Board. On the back side of the Vision Board you just created, draw pictures or use words to describe what life will be like if you DON'T work hard to stay in recovery. In other words, can you imagine some of the bad potential scenarios? Draw them out on the back or use words to describe them.

For example, Justin used pictures to remind himself of the following possibilities:

- My feeling of guilt and shame will probably get worse.
- I might get so depressed I can't do my schoolwork.
- I don't think my girlfriend will want to keep dating me.
- I'm not sure I'd feel good about getting married.
- My future wife may feel really betrayed if I can't stop.
- My kids _might_ find out, just like I did with MY dad.
- I might isolate myself more and lose friends.

Anger Release

Sometimes you might be holding onto anger that you don't know what to do with. It starts building up and you realize you're walking around just fuming inside. Maybe someone did something that hurt you. It could be really unfair. Doesn't matter what happened, the anger buildup can become a trigger.

Find things you can actively do with the anger. For example, Paulo got super angry about his father. Life seemed unfair. He listed the following things he could do whenever the anger built up inside:

- Go to the driving range and hit golf balls for an hour.
- Hit on the punching bag in the garage.
- Smash ice cubes on the driveway with a hammer.
- Go to the batting cages and hit baseballs.
- Sit in the car and scream out loud about how I'm angry.
- Go run hard for 15 minutes around the block.
- Call my mentor and tell him about why I'm so angry.
- Go to the Rec Center with my friend and do cardio.
- Get over to the skate park and ride hard for a couple hours.

Mental Replay

Go back and think about the last time you crossed your bottom line. Don't just sit there feeling bad about yourself. This is a chance to brainstorm— how could you have dodged that slip? Think about what was going on and ask yourself, "What else could I have done?" There's got to be some other choices you could've made. Maybe there's some tools you haven't tried or buddies you could've called for backup? Find a quiet place and write down a few tools you could've used at that time, or how you could have handled things differently. Write down several options in the spaces provided.

1.____

2.____

3.____

4.____

Now shut your eyes and replay that moment right before things went sideways. Get all the details in your head, nice and slow. Shake it up and picture a different response — something other than slipping. Run through this new scene repeatedly in your head. Really see it and feel it.

After you've got that new scenario memorized, go talk it out with someone you trust, someone who's got your back. This is about changing your strategy ahead of time, so when you're in a tight spot you've got new options ready.

Artwork Replay

Just like the "mental replay," think about making a picture that shows off all the good options you could take, instead of giving in to temptation. Spend some time putting together a collage or poster that really highlights positive responses, instead of slipping. Illustrate some of the tools or weapons that work well for you. You could sketch yourself utilizing any of the tools or weapons mentioned in this armory.

Make sure your artwork is super detailed. When you look at it, you should be able to clearly picture what you are doing. Don't rush it. The more you dive into these positive visuals, the more you'll find yourself naturally leaning into them when you're feeling the urge to do something sexual. Once you're proud of your creation, show it off to your group, a close friend, or maybe a mentor. Ask them to guess your strategy from the artwork.

Combat Prep

This tool asks you to think ahead about preparing for combat. Just like soldiers out in the field, you need to be prepared for battle. Picture those moments when you're about to do something you might regret. In other words, think about times you've been really tempted to cross your bottom lines. Got it? Now, think about what you could do in those moments. Take a few minutes to think it through. What are four or five moves you're going to make when you're in that spot? Jot these down. Keep it straightforward and tailor it to those times you usually find yourself slipping.

Elijah came up with this "combat prep" for when he's bored after school and tempted:

- Text Collin from Valor group and talk about what's going on.
- Head outside and shoot hoops.
- Swing by Trevor's house to see if he wants to hang out.
- Spend some time fixing up my bike in the garage, and crank up the tunes for half an hour.
- Check in with Collin again to talk about how the afternoon went.

Now think about weapons or tools you can use for YOUR temptations. Write some specific things on the chart for those moments.

My Combat Prep:

1. ______________________________

____

____

2. ______________________________

____

____

3. ______________________________

____

____

4. ______________________________

____

____

5. ______________________________

____

____

Combat Drills

This tool is like your combat prep, only it's a dry run practice. Revisit your combat prep and make sure you know what moves you're going to make when the urge to slip happens. Once you've got your strategy down, it's time to run a combat drill.

Work on your Combat Drills even when you're not struggling. These moves need to be second nature. Set aside some time and go through each step when you're not struggling. Pick a day to run through your combat drills so you're mentally ready to tackle the next challenge.

For example, Tyler decided to do Combat Drills on Thursday afternoon. Here's what he planned:

- Text Ethan from Valor group to touch base.
- Head over to Jason's house for XBOX.
- Meet Jordan after school to get help with homework.
- Check in my phone with my mom at 9:30pm.

Tokens

A token is an item to help you get grounded. It's something that keeps your head on straight, helps you chill out, and reminds you about recovery. It could literally be anything that is meaningful to you - a coin, a pebble from a hike, something to toss in your pocket, a necklace, a wrist band, or maybe a nick-nack you keep on a shelf.

Pick something that's got a story to you - something sentimental. Show it to your best friend, your parents, a mentor, your group, your roommate, or anyone who is supporting you. Get them to hold the token and say positive words about you. Later, when you're holding the token, you can remember what they've said. Whenever you're feeling off, just take a minute to hold this token.

Hit the Style

This tool requires you to quickly analyze what "style" of addiction you're sliding into. Go back and read the workbook material if needed. Remember that each style has a different chemical your brain releases. Here's a quick review:

- **Satiation**
  This is when you want to act out because you need to relax and chill from all the stress or anxiety in your life.

- **Arousal**
  This is when you want to act out because you need some excitement or adventure from the boredom or monotony you might be feeling.

- **Fantasy**
  This is when you want to act out because you need an escape from reality, the pressures of life, or the memory of something that might have happened.

Here are some possible ideas.

- **Satiation**
  Liam listed the following ideas to help him calm down and chill.

  - Lay down and listen to soft music, taking deep breaths.
  - Sit in the jacuzzi with my brother.
  - Ask my mom to scratch my back.

- **Arousal**
  Ethan listed the following ideas when he is bored and needs adventure.

  - Play pick-up ball at the park.
  - Walk around the mall with friends.
  - Go to a football game with guys in my church group.

- **Fantasy**
  Oliver listed the following ideas when he needs an escape from reality.

  - Read my favorite book.
  - Work on my go-cart in the garage.
  - Write or play some new music on the piano.

Now think about what might work for you:

Satiation

Arousal

Fantasy

Energy Shift

Remember we talked about how your brain slides into old ruts when you slip, and floods your bloodstream with chemicals? That's a big reason why it's so hard to quit using porn.

A tool called "Energy Shift" is basically doing stuff that changes your body's chemistry. It's a cool trick to shift those urges before they get out of hand. Think about activities that could change your chemistry in a good way. These would be things that change how you feel physically. For example, things like sports, hiking, walking outside, hanging out with friends, going to the skate park, or social activities. This isn't about distraction—it's about giving your brain a new kind of rush - the healthy kind.

Here are some examples of how Abe would use Energy Shift to change things up. Notice that each of Abe's items change the physical sensations in his body.:

- Jump into the cold swimming pool.
- Ride my bike to Nate's house.
- Jog for ten minutes non-stop.
- Ask my mom for a hug.

Distraction

When facing sexual urges, sometimes you just need some distraction. Fun activities can act as a buffer. Whether it's working on a hobby, spending time with friends, or learning something new, distracting experiences pull you away from tempting thoughts.

Take a few minutes to write down a list of "distracting" activities when you're struggling. Remember this can be anything that's fun, engaging, or simply causes you to redirect your mind.

Distraction Activities

AIM

This weapon has three steps you should memorize. You've got to run through these steps every time you feel that struggle to cross your bottom lines. It requires a bit of detective work about what's going on inside your head.

Step 1: ADMIT

You must admit that you are struggling and overwhelmed. Simply be honest and admit you're struggling. "This is really hard right now."

Step 2: IDENTIFY

Try to figure out what's underneath the current struggle. What is bugging you? This is about spotting what's stirring up the storm inside. Could be something on an emotional level, so you've got to get real with yourself. What's the trigger and where's it coming from?

Step 3: MOVE

Once you "identify" what's under the struggle, it's time to move. If you're feeling lonely, then go find your friends. If you got rejected today, then go find someone who understands you. Don't keep it bottled up. Talk about it with your group or a counselor to find ways to resolve it. The whole point of using the AIM tool is to help you address anything that's causing a trigger.

Action Plan

Make sure there are no chinks in your armor. The Action Plan is a way for you to put pieces in place to win the war against your problems with porn. Your action plan will focus on the key items for overall success. The goal is to keep everything in your life balanced. Discuss your strategy with your counselor, coach, parents, Valor group, or a reliable mentor you trust.

BOTTOM LINES

(behaviors you're trying to stop)

ELECTRONICS PLAN

(includes TV, gaming, phones)

AMMO BOX

(include the date you finish it)

REACH OUT

(List names you can call)

____

____

____

____

____

ACCOUNTABILITY PARTNER

(list two people you could ask)

____

____

____

____

MENTOR

(trusted male adult who is not your parent)

____

____

____

SPIRITUAL MENTOR
(pastor or leader from church)

____

____

____

____

EXERCISE

____

____

____

____

SLEEP & REST

____

____

____

____

SOCIAL ACTIVITIES

____

____

____

____

SPIRITUAL ACTIVITIES

HOBBIES

SCHOOL & GRADES

NOTES

BHLAST

This tool helps you spot the triggers that are causing you trouble. Remember, triggers are anything that kick-starts your sexual thoughts and leads you to cross bottom lines. If you can figure out the trigger, you'll have a better chance at avoiding slips. So, when you're feeling tempted, just hit BHLAST! Here's how it breaks down:

B - BOREDOM

H - HUNGRY

L - LONELY

A - ANGRY

S - STRESSED

T - TIRED

BOREDOM

You might find yourself with nothing to do, or forced to do things that aren't fun (like homework or chores). If this is the case, find something fun and entertaining to do as soon as you can.

HUNGRY

Make sure you're eating. If you're running on empty, your brain's not going to think clearly. Go get a snack. But it's not always about food. Ever feel like you're craving solid friendships or hungry for some affection? If this is the case, go feed your need!

LONELY

There might be times you feel isolated and lonely. You might have a legitimate need for companionship. This could also mean there's simply no one around – you are alone. If this is your situation, go find people and get connected!

ANGRY

You might be upset or frustrated. It doesn't matter why or what it's about, anger carries a lot of energy that can set temptations into motion. If anger is a trigger for you, go find a way to release the energy.

STRESSED

You might be overwhelmed with life. School pressure can be intense. You might feel buried by so much to do. If this is the situation, pause and find a way to chill out.

TIRED

This is definitely about getting enough sleep. When you are sleep-deprived it's hard to focus. It's also important to take breaks during the day when you're physically or emotionally worn out. Learn to pace yourself. Find a way to rest by taking a nap, going to bed early, or simply avoiding emotional drama.

Once you can identify any of the BHLAST clues… go find ways to resolve these triggers.

Accountability Mirror

With a stack of post-it notes, write down your goals and stick them on your bathroom or bedroom mirror. Pause when looking in the mirror to remind yourself. Read the goals out loud to yourself. Watch your facial expression and speak to yourself about why this goal is important.

Similarly, write down any tools or weapons you are planning to practice this week. Pause when looking in the mirror and imagine you are using this tool or weapon in real time. Watch your facial expression and speak with confidence about the strong effort you are making.

THE JOURNEY AHEAD

You're now equipped with tools and weapons to use in your fight against pornography and sexual compulsions or addictions. Keep referring to this Armory to help you throughout your recovery.

Your Valor group will be filled with new experiences and information for you to be successful. Work with your group, counselor or coach, and mentors through the Valor workbooks:

- **Workbook 1: Squire**
- **Workbook 2: Archer**
- **Workbook 3: Sergeant**
- **Workbook 4: Captain**
- **Workbook 5: Knight**

Guidebooks:

- **The Armory**
- **Mentor's Guide**
- **Parent's Guide**

REFERENCES

The Valor series materials were developed and influenced through clinical observation, professional research, collegial collaboration, and personal experience having worked in social services with adolescents over 30 years. The following organizations and resources were helpful in the development of this program:

- **SASH**
  (Society for the Advancement of Sexual Health)

- **IITAP**
  (International Institute for Treatment Addiction Professionals)

- **LifeSTAR**
  (Pornography and Sex Addiction Programming)

- **AASAT**
  (American Association for Sex Addiction Therapy)

- **AACC**
  (American Association of Christian Counselors)

Bowlby, J. (1988). *A secure base: Parent-child attachment and Healthy Human Development*. Basic Books.

Carnes, P. (1989). *Contrary to love: Helping the sexual addict*. Hazelden.

Carnes, P., & Carnes, P. (2001). *Out of the shadows: Understanding sexual addiction*. Hazelden Information & Edu.

Carnes, P., Delmonico, D., & Griffin, E. (2001). *In the Shadows of the Net: Breaking Free of Compulsive Online Sexual Behavior*. Hazelden.

Carnes, P., & Schwartz, B. K. (2010). *Facing the shadow: Starting sexual and relationship recovery: A gentle path to beginning recovery from sex addiction*. Gentle Path Press.

Carnes, P., Delmonico, D., & Griffin, E. (2001). *In The shadows of the net: Breaking free of compulsive online sexual behavior*. Hazelden.

Clear, J. (2018). *Atomic habits: An easy yet proven way to build good habits and break bad ones: Tiny changes, remarkable results*. Avery, an imprint of Penguin Random House.

Cline, F., & Fay, J. (2020). *Parenting with Love & Logic: Teaching Children Responsibility*. NavPress.

Diamond, D., Blatt, S. J., & Lichtenberg, J. D. (2014). *Attachment and sexuality*. Routledge.

Flores, P. J. (2004). *Addiction as an attachment disorder*. Jason Aronson.

Fortify: A step toward recovery. (2013). O.W.L. Publishing.

Gray, D., & Olson, T. (2012). *LifeSTAR Addiction Recovery Workbooks*. LifeSTAR Network.

Gray, D., & Olson, T. (2005). *Surviving Withdrawal - Laying the Groundwork for a Lasting Recovery*. LifeSTAR Network.

Home. Fight the New Drug. (2024, May 6). https://fightthenewdrug.org/

Kastleman, M. B. (2001). *The drug of the New Millennium: The Science of how internet pornography radically alters the human brain and body*. Granite Pub.

Katehakis, A., & Schore, A. N. (2016). *Sex addiction as affect dysregulation: A neurobiologically informed holistic treatment.* W.W. Norton & Company.

Laaser, M. R., & Laaser, M. R. (2004). *Healing the wounds of sexual addiction.* Zondervan.

Laaser, M. (1999). *Talking to your Kids about Sex.* Random House Publishing.

Mulligan, C. (2013). *How to recover from cyber pornography addiction: The teen cyber pornography.* Lulu Com.

Pollack, W. S. (1999). *Real boys: Rescuing our sons from the myths of boyhood.* H. Holt.

Wasserman, B. (1998). *Feeling good again: A workbook for children who have been sexually abused.* Safer Society Press.

Weiss, R., & Sack, D. (2015). *Sex addiction 101: A basic guide to healing from sex, Porn, and Love addiction.* Health Communications, Inc.

Weiss, R., & Schneider, J. P. (2014). *Closer together, further apart: The effect of Technology and the internet on parenting, work, and relationships.* Gentle Path Press.

Weiss, R., & Schneider, J. P. (2015). *Always turned on: Facing sex addiction in the Digital age.* Gentle Path Press.

Wilson, G. (2017). *Your brain on porn - internet pornography and the emerging science of addiction.* Commonwealth Publishing.

Wright, L. B., & Loiselle, M. B. (1997). *Back on track: Boys dealing with sexual abuse.* Safer Society Press.